Originally published as *Superbeesjes. De beste mama's en papa's*
in Belgium and the Netherlands by Clavis Uitgeverij, 2020
English translation from the Dutch by Clavis Publishing Inc., New York

Visit us on the Web at www.clavis-publishing.com.

Super Animals. The Best Mommies and Daddies
written by Reina Ollivier and Karel Claes,
and illustrated by Steffie Padmos

ISBN 978-1-60537-627-1

This book was printed in November 2020 at Nikara,
M. R. Štefánika 858/25, 963 01 Krupina, Slovakia.

First Edition
10 9 8 7 6 5 4 3 2 1

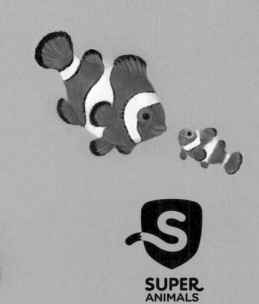

SUPER ANIMALS

THE BEST
MOMMIES AND DADDIES

Written by **Reina Ollivier** & **Karel Claes**
Illustrated by **Steffie Padmos**

Clavis
NEW YORK

Mommies and daddies are very important.
They take care of you and teach you how to become independent.
Do animal mommies and daddies do that as well?

Some don't, like the cuckoo.
She lays her eggs in the nests of other birds.
Then, she flies away, without even looking back.

But other animals are very caring toward their little ones.
American flamingos divide the tasks between mommy and daddy.
With emperor penguins, daddy hatches the egg.
And with orangutans, mommy does all the work.
There are lots of animals that are excellent mommies or daddies.
Let's visit them together!

CONTENTS

EMPEROR PENGUIN

We live in one of the coldest places on earth, at the very bottom of the globe. And yet, we manage to hatch an egg in the icy snow and give our chicks enough warmth.

Who am I?

Name: emperor penguin
Class: birds

Size: 43-50 inches
(110-130 centimeters); males and
females are the same size;
males are a little heavier

Best mommy and daddy
Daddy hatches the egg
for two months without eating
anything. Then, mommy takes
care of the chick on her own
for a month. Afterwards, daddy
and mommy take turns
getting food.

Legs:
2 short legs with
webbed claws.

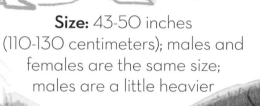

sharp **claws** give
grip on the ice

Habitat: ice fields on the South Pole (Antarctica)

Food:
fish, krill, squid

Speed:
On land, I waddle forward slowly, or I let myself slide
downhill on my belly. In the water, I'm a good swimmer.

0   6 mph   60

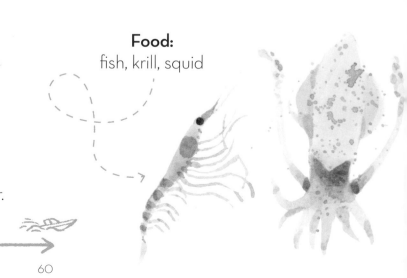

Enemies:
Big birds of prey like the **south polar skua**
often attack young penguins.

orcas   sharks   leopard seals

crooked beak with
orange stripe

on the side of the head,
a **golden-yellow spot**
that goes on as far as the neck

short wings serve
to keep my **balance**
on the land

I have a **layer of fat** that's
1.5 inches (4 centimeters) thick,
and an impenetrable **plumage.**
That way, I'm **protected**
against the biting wind
and the freezing water.

Only emperor penguins hatch an **egg** in the **winter.**
The winter in Antarctica lasts from April till October.
That's a lot of dark months without sun.

From January to March, I look for **food** in the ocean,
day and night. I can dive up to 1640 feet (500 meters)
deep and stay underwater for 20 minutes. With my paws,
I regulate how deep I want to **swim.** I steer to the left or to
the right with my short tail. My wings are used as paddles.

Starting in April, I move away from the pack ice with
other penguins. We take a **long trip** to a **breeding ground**
inland. Sometimes, more than 62 miles (100 kilometers)
away! We breed together with **thousands** of others.

All penguins stand **close together** in a circle.
Whoever is standing on the outer edge slowly
moves to the middle, where it's nice and warm.
That way, we **take turns** enjoying the **warmth.**

At the end of May, mommy lays an egg of approximately 1 pound (470 grams) that she passes on to daddy. He doesn't sit on it, like other birds. He shoves the egg onto his paws and covers it with a skin flap. You call that a pouch. Laying the egg demanded a lot from mommy's powers. She returns to the sea to restock her fat supply. For two months, daddy hatches the egg without eating anything. He loses almost 44 pounds (20 kilograms).

The eggshell is very hard. I peck for two entire days to get out of the egg. Daddy gives me warmth and milk. He tells me that mommy will come soon. And that's right. She has got a tummy full of food. Every day, she throws up a little food for me. I can eat that easily.

In the meantime, daddy goes to the sea for four weeks to eat. Afterwards, mommy and daddy take turns caring for me. Mid-October, I huddle together with the other chicks in the nursery. There, we sit together warm and safe while our parents get food. In December, I have a fully developed plumage and I can take care of myself.

FOX

I appear in a lot of stories because I'm smart and sly. That's necessary when you have to find food for your wife and children. Don't I look handsome with my red fur and thick tail?

Who am I?

Name: fox
Class: mammals

Size:
18-35.5 inches
(45-90 centimeters) long
plus a tail of 12.5-22 inches
(32-56 centimeters);
males are a little bigger
than females

4 sharp canines
and **firm jaws**
to chew meat

Legs:
4 high legs

Food:
eats everything he finds: little mammals,
birds, eggs, fruit, leftovers

Habitat: forests, rugged grasslands, parks, and
wild places in the city; just about everywhere in
the northern hemisphere. The fox didn't originally
live in Australia, but was introduced there by men.

Speed:
My average speed is 6 miles per hour.
Over a short distance, I reach a top speed of 31 miles per hour.

0   31 mph   60

Best mommy and daddy
Mommy stays with
the young foxes in the nest
and daddy brings all the food.

Enemies:

eagles   bobcats   wolves   bears   pumas

very **limber,**
can swim very well
and jump over enclosures
that are 6 feet
(2 meters) high

makes **a lot of noises:**
screams, howls, and
barks like a dog

triangular head
with **pointed snout,**
long whiskers,
and **pointy ears**

thick, **fluffy tail**
that touches the ground
when the fox is standing still

I'm a **shy** animal and I rarely show myself. During the day, I sleep, and **during the night,** I go **hunting.** When I see a prey, I sneak closer on my toes. I push myself off with my hind legs and jump on top of it. I can hear animals moving beneath the ground, even from 16 feet (5 meters) away. Then, I dig **very fast** to catch them. I **hear and smell exceptionally well.**

My partner and I mark our **territory** by **peeing** on clearly visible places. The powerful smell tells other animals that we live here and that they aren't welcome.

I **adapt everywhere** and eat anything. That's why you can even find me in big **cities.** There, I eat mice, rats, and cats, and I grab food from trash cans.

It's spring. My three brothers have already left the house. My sister and I prefer to stay with mommy and daddy. We returned to an old burrow for the birth of my new brothers and sisters. Most of the time, we sleep hidden between the bushes. But when little foxes are born, it's safer beneath the ground.

Mommy and daddy clean the old burrow. With their front legs, they scrape away earth, and with their hind legs, they kick it a few feet away from the burrow. They trample down the earth, so food can be placed on it. We also use it as a playground.

New-born cubs are blind and deaf, but they have soft fur. Their tail is as long as one half of their body. Mommy stays close to the young foxes during the first weeks. She keeps them warm and lets them drink her milk. Daddy gets food for mommy, so she stays strong and healthy. I help with taking care of the little ones.

After a month, the little foxes come outside. We play together a lot. Foxes are fond of wild games. Sometimes, mommy or daddy bring a little ball from a garden or a golf course. It's always fun and games in our fox family!

ORANGUTAN

I swing from branch to branch and I'm the biggest animal that lives in trees. I teach my little one everything about the forest. There's a lot to learn and that's why he stays with me for eight years. No other animal takes care of their child for such a long time.

Who am I?

Name: orangutan
Class: mammals

the arms are one and a half times as **long** as the legs

Arms and legs:
2 long, muscular arms and two short, bent legs; 4 long, pliable fingers and toes plus a shorter thumb and toe; no tail

Size:
males up to 55 inches (140 centimeters); females up to 47 inches (120 centimeters)

Best mommy
Mommy takes care of her child all by herself for 8 years.

Food:
fruit, plants, insects (ants and termites), birds' eggs

Habitat:
the rainforests of Sumatra and Borneo islands

Speed:

0   3 mph

60

Enemies:

tigers   clouded   crocodiles   people
          leopards

People cut trees and build fields and roads. By doing that, they make our habitat smaller. They catch young orangutans to sell them as a pet.

Orang and *hutan* are words from Malaysia. They mean *person* and *forest*. So, an orangutan is **someone from the forest.**

My **arms** are very **muscular,** so they can easily carry my weight. I move slowly because I take **much time** to gather **food.**

32 **teeth**
just like humans

males have **cheek pads** between their eyes and ears; they have bigger throat pouches than the females and a beard

Next to the gorilla and the chimpanzee, we're **the biggest apes.** We're seven times as **strong** as a human. We live alone much more often than other monkey species.

I know exactly **where and when** which kind of **fruit** is **ripe** in the rainforest. I also use **tools** to get food. Don't you think that's **smart?** I can bring **food** to my mouth **with my hands and my feet.** That comes in handy when I'm hanging in a tree and want to eat juicy fruit. I use my **lips** to **touch** food before I bite into it.

My mommy is with me day and night. The first two years of my life, I hold on tight to her reddish-brown fur. We swing through the trees together and we sleep in the same nest. Afterwards, I hold her hand when I walk on the branches. My older sister and other mommies also help me. Sometimes, mommy acts like a bridge and I walk over her arms and shoulders to the next branch.

She teaches me which plants are edible. And how I can eat the flesh of the durian, a prickly fruit native to my habitat, without having the spines hurt me. You think the durian stinks, but I love it!

I pay close attention to the way mommy uses a branch. She uses it to get fruit from a tree and take honey from the bees. And she churns up nests, so I can eat ants and termites.

Mommy shows me how to make a nest in a tree. We braid branches into a firm bottom. In it, we put a layer of fine branches and leaves. A soft mattress!

At the lake, mommy always makes a bowl using her hands. I imitate her and can drink fresh water like that. Until I'm eight, she also breastfeeds me. She's my super mommy!

CLOWN FISH

We live in or under a sea anemone and we really like it there. It's where we lay our eggs, which we can guard well. That's why we're also called anemone fish. Can you guess why they call us clown fish?

Who am I?

Name: clown fish
Class: fish

Size:
3-4.5 inches
(8-11 centimeters);
females clearly bigger
than males

Fins:
2 dorsal fins, 2 pectoral fins,
2 ventral fins, an anal fin,
and a tail fin.

Best mommy and daddy
Daddy guards the eggs
that mommy lays. Together,
they flap their fins, so the eggs
get oxygenated water.

The three white **stripes**
on our body make people
think of the face of a **clown.**

Food:
algae, plankton, plants,
little marine animals (mollusks
and crustaceans)

Habitat:
the warm water of the tropical
coral reefs in the east of Asia

Speed:

O   4 mph   60

Enemies:

big fish   sharks

All clown fish are **born as males.** The biggest male becomes **a female** when there's no female in the group.

An **anemone** has **poisonous tentacles** that can kill me. When I pick a beautiful anemone, I dance around it. I touch it with my fins first. Afterwards, with other parts of my body. That way, **a mucus layer** is formed on my scales that **protects** me against the poison.

The anemone and I help each other. I keep him clean by eating food particles. When I swim around the anemone, I bring oxygen in the water and I supply food. I chase away fish that eat anemones. In exchange, I get to live there. And with its poison, the anemone kills the fish that want to attack me.

I'm a female. I live with a male
and a few younger male fish.
Our **size** indicates how **important** we are.
The female is always the biggest fish
of the group.

I stay safely near my anemone,
because I'm **not a good swimmer.**

Mommy and daddy search for an egg-laying place close to the anemone.
At full moon, mommy swims over their chosen spot a few times.
She lays 400 to 1500 eggs there. Daddy follows her to fertilize the eggs.

Afterwards, daddy attentively looks at the eggs.
He picks the bad ones and eats them,
because a rotten egg can spoil all other eggs.
Every day, my daddy checks the eggs.
Daddy also flaps his fins toward the eggs.
Mommy helps him with that.
That way, a lot of air gets into the water.
That's good for the growth of the eggs.

After a week, we get out of the eggs as transparent larvae.
We swim to the moonlight and let ourselves drift away
on the water. We feed on plankton and don't need daddy
and mommy anymore. After another week, we get color
and pick our own anemone.

AMERICAN FLAMINGO

We live together in big groups. We eat, fly, and breed together. But each pair builds their own nest in the mud. In it, one egg is laid, which we surround with great care.

Who am I?

Name: American flamingo
Class: birds

pinkish-red to orange plumage with lighter feathers on the back

little pale-yellow **eyes**

long, supple neck

Legs:
2 long, slim legs with webbed toes

long wings with a wingspan of 5 feet (1.5 meters)

Size: 47-55 inches (120-140 centimeters); males a little bigger than females

wide **crooked beak,** pink with black tip

Food: worms, insects, little shellfish, little crustaceans (shrimps and little lobsters), plants, algae

Habitat: shallow waters at the shore, mud flats, and salt lakes in the Caribbean area

Speed:
We wade slowly through the water. When we take flight, we run a few steps first. Then, we open our wings and soar through the sky. When we land, we also run a few steps.

0   37 mph   60

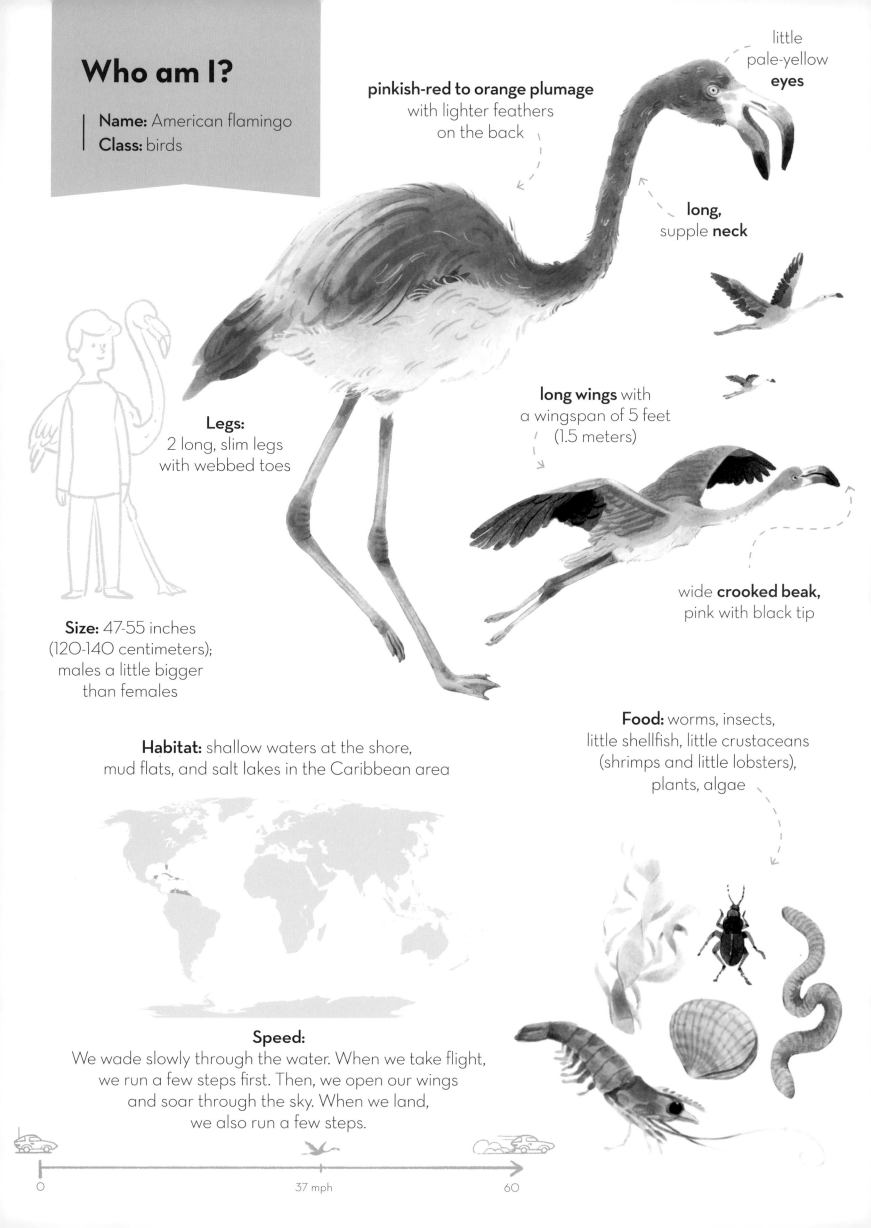

Enemies:

jaguars   birds of prey   raccoons

Birds of prey and raccoons steal the eggs
and attack young flamingos.

Best mommy and daddy
Mommy and daddy hatch
the egg alternately
in the nest. They both
give milk to their chick.

We live in **big groups**
of thousands of birds and
protect each other. Because
when I'm looking for food
with my head in the water,
I'm easy prey.

With my beak upside-down,
I rummage through the mud. That way,
I scoop up food. My **beak** works like
a **sieve.** The water streams out of it
and the food stays inside.

When there's **no food** anymore,
we fly with the group to a **different
place** at night. During the flight,
I keep my long **neck and legs stretched.**
Under my spread wings, you see
black feathers. Those are invisible
when I'm not flying.

I rest on one leg.
I bend the **other leg** under
my body to **warm** my toes.
I turn the front part of my body
towards the **wind.** It blows over
my **feathers** and puts them
into place.

I get my **pink-orange color** by eating algae and little lobsters.
There's a coloring agent in them that you can also find inside carrots.

Mommy and daddy build a hill in the mud.
They hollow it out, so an egg fits into it.
The high mud edge protects the egg
against water and strong heat.

Taking turns, mommy and
daddy protect the nest.
Every now and then, they stretch
their legs, spread their wings,
and clean their feathers
to relax for a moment.
Sometimes, they carefully
turn their egg around
with their beak.

After a month, they hear ticking in the eggshell.
That's me! They watch tensely how I try my best
to get out. That can take 24 to 36 hours. They
caress me with their beak and smooth out
my greyish-white down feathers.

Mommy and daddy both give me milk.
That crop milk is very powerful food.
After a week, I'm strong enough to step
out of the nest. Mommy and daddy always
stay nearby. They make sure that nothing
happens to me. They bring me food
until I get real feathers. Then, I'm
11 weeks old, and my straight beak
gradually grows crooked.

RED KANGAROO

I jump faster than any other animal. While jumping, I use less energy than when I'm running. And in the heat of Australia, it's important to save energy. Especially when you have to take care of the little ones all by yourself!

Who am I?

Name: red kangaroo
Class: mammals

Best mommy and daddy
When mommy is pregnant, she also carries a baby kangaroo in her pouch and takes care of a slightly older little one at the same time.

Size:
males up to 79 inches (200 centimeters) plus a tail of 47 inches (120 centimeters); females up to 41 inches (105 centimeters) plus a tail of 33.5 inches (85 centimeters)

long, pointy ears

Legs:
2 smaller front legs and 2 muscular hind legs

only **females** have a **pouch**

Habitat:
open grasslands with a few trees in the dry inland of Australia

Food:
plants, mostly grass

Speed:
Usually 12 miles per hour, but I can jump up to 43 miles per hour.

0   43 mph   60

Enemies:

dingoes   eagles

There are **more than 50 species** of kangaroos living in Australia, but **we're** the **biggest ones.** We live in **small groups** and we can survive for **months without water.** We have **few enemies** and **enough to eat.** Farmers cut down forests and made meadows for their cattle, which gave us more room to eat!

I'm a real **beefcake.** Half of my body consists of muscles. The strongest ones are in my hind legs and tail. I can **jump** 9 yards (8 meters) **far and** 10 feet (3 meters) **high.** When there's a **threat,** I stomp on the ground with my **hind legs.** My shorter **front legs** are strong as well. I use them to **fight.** I can box like a human. Sometimes, I lean on my tail for a moment and give a **good kicking** with both hind legs.

my very **muscular tail** is a kind of third hind leg that ensures **balance** while jumping

Because it's so **hot** in Australia, we take a rest **during the day in the shadows.** We start to **graze** only when **the sun goes down.** Sometimes, I wet my front legs with **saliva.** That **cools me down!**

My mommy is almost always pregnant.
Sometimes, a new baby in her belly has to stop
growing until there's room in the pouch.

After 33 days of growing, I push myself through
mommy's thick fur to her pouch. I'm blind, bald,
and barely .8 inch (2 centimeters) big. My hind legs
are only stumps. But I smell where the milk is
and suck onto one of mommy's nipples.

Mommy has four nipples with two kinds of
milk. Because every now and then, my older
brother puts his snout in the pouch to drink
as well. He does that until he's one year old.

Mommy's pouch is a safe place. I stay there for three months and show my little head occasionally. I also use the pouch as a toilet. When it gets too filthy in there, mommy puts her snout in the pouch. With her tongue, she licks up dirt, urine, and feces.

Mommy talks to me by means of click sounds. She protects me and my brother against attackers and she can growl like an angry dog. She kicks away dingoes with her legs. My mommy can do everything!

43

ZEBRA FINCH

We always stay together. We live in a dry area and wait to lay eggs until it has rained a lot. That's the best time to raise our young ones.

Who am I?

Name: zebra finch
Class: birds

males have orange spots
on the cheeks and **dots** on the sides;
the **females** are a lot **less colorful**

Size: 4-4.5 inches
(10-11 centimeters)

only **males sing,**
females don't

males have **black-and-white
stripes on their neck,**
like the skin of a zebra

Legs:
2 orange legs

Habitat:
dry grasslands of Australia and Indonesia,
with a bush or a tree here and there

Food:
mainly seeds of
all kinds of grass,
complete with insects
(ants and termites)

Speed:

0   18 mph   60

Enemies:

 giant lizards

 rats

 snakes

 birds of prey

crows

 marsupials of prey

young zebra finches have a **black beak, females** have an **orange beak, older males** have **red beaks**

Best mommy and daddy
Mommy and daddy take care of the nest and the little ones together. Daddy is a patient vocal coach for his sons.

Every male has **his personal song** and sings it to his little ones. The **boys** just imitate their daddy at first. Afterwards, they add **new sounds.** As soon as a zebra finch is happy about his melody, he sings his **own song for the rest of his life. Females** don't sing, but they do **recognize the songs** of the males.

I can live **without water for a long time.** But when I find water, I like to take a **bath.**

We have **many enemies** and think it's **safer** to live in a **big group.** Approximately 50 families have their nest in the same neighborhood. We also peck our **food** off the ground **together.**

We are **very colorful** and **easily expand** our family. And we sing **beautiful songs.** That's why people tamed us for the first time 150 years ago and put us **in cages.**

Mommy and daddy make their nest in a briar patch or in a tree. Mommy picks the place and daddy brings most of the material. He builds the base with grass stems and mommy makes it soft with feathers and bits of fluff. She lays five eggs in it.

Mommy and daddy alternately hatch the eggs. At night, they cozily sit on the nest together. Daddy chases away anyone who dares to come close.

After two weeks, the eggs have hatched.
Mommy and daddy take turns staying with us.
The other one gets food. Mommy and daddy
only eat grass seeds, but for us, they bring insects.
Those make us grow big and strong faster.

After three weeks, we get to fly away. Yet we often return to the nest in the evening because it's so cozy with mommy and daddy. We're always welcome. When we're 35 days old, mommy and daddy have taught us enough and we can live on our own.

WOLF

In books, it's often told that we're dangerous animals. *Little Red Riding Hood and the Wolf* is the most well-known example of that. Actually, we're scared of people and we stay away from them. We care a lot about our family and about the other wolves in our group.

Who am I?

Name: wolf
Class: mammals

wide head with **small ears**
that are set wide apart

thick fur in the **winter** that offers a lot of
warmth in freezing temperatures

Size:
males 39-59 inches
(100-150 centimeters) long
and a tail of 12-20 inches
(30-50 centimeters);
females are a little smaller

very **strong jaws**
and four slightly
crooked **canines** of 1 inch
(2.5 centimeters) long

Legs:
4 powerful,
long legs

Best mommy and daddy
Mommy stays in the nest with her little
ones for three weeks and in the meantime, daddy takes care of the food.

Habitat: forests, grasslands, mountains,
and dry areas in the northern hemisphere

Food:
deer, wild boar, bears, moose,
bison, mountain goats, beavers,
hares, birds, little rodents

Speed:
I run 5-6 miles per hour, but I can
sprint up to 40 miles per hour.

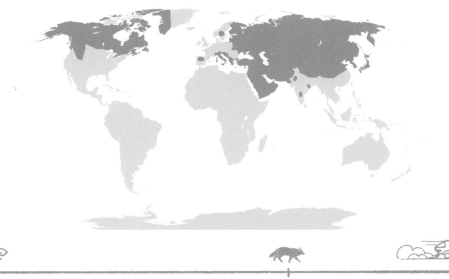

0   40 mph   60

I'm the **ancestor of the dog.** Just like him, I pick up **high sounds** that people can't hear. I can also **smell and see very well,** even when it's **pitch-black.**

bears pumas tigers wolves people

We pass on **information** to others **by howling and taking on certain postures.** When I'm **angry,** my fur stands straight up. I show my teeth and growl loudly. When I'm **scared,** I put my tail between my hind legs, bow my head and cry softly. You can hear my **howling** 6 miles (10 kilometers) **away.**

I'm a **carnivore** that **hunts** big prey **in a group.** We mostly attack **young, old or wounded animals.** They can't move very fast and we can catch them quicker.

Our wolf family is called a **pack.** It consists of **a male and a female** that are in charge. Apart from that, there are the little ones that were born this year and their older brothers and sisters. Sometimes, other wolves get to join too, but they have to listen to the **two leaders.** Wolf packs **defend their territory** and sometimes attack other packs.

I'm happy that I'm part of our wolf pack, because we make up a very close family. Mommy and daddy stay together their entire life. Soon, new cubs will be born again in the wolf den. Mommy and daddy have appropriated a fox burrow together. It's easier to use an existing burrow than having to dig out everything themselves.

Every year in April, mommy gives birth to 4 to 6 cubs. They weigh approximately 1 pound (0.5 kilogram) each and they're still deaf and blind. But they can smell and feel well. Mommy gives milk to the cubs and keeps them close to her. Daddy goes hunting and drags food inside. In the beginning, the little ones only drink milk. After a month, they lick up half-digested food from mommy's mouth. The other wolves and I help daddy with bringing food. That way, mommy can stay with the cubs the entire time.

When the little ones are two months old, they come along
to the playground. There, daddy teaches them how to behave
in the pack. Sometimes, he's really tough on them. But we love
to roll around together with mommy and daddy.

YELLOW SEAHORSE

We're so happy we found each other! We don't like to travel and always live in the same place. And we get a lot of little seahorses. Doesn't that sound like a fairytale?

Who am I?

Name: yellow seahorse
Class: fish

eyes move **independently** of each other

long snout to **suck up** food

Size:
3-7 inches
(7-17 centimeters)

Fins:
a dorsal fin and
two pectoral fins that
stand right behind
the eyes

the **male** has
a **brood pouch**

Habitat:
shallow saltwater in tropical areas in Asia

Food:
plankton, little crustaceans,
newborn fish

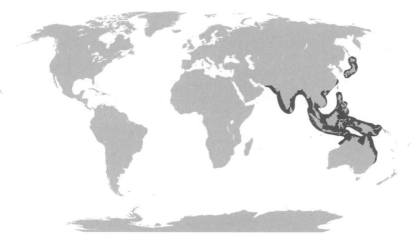

Speed:
I swim very slowly: barely 2 yards (2 meters) per hour.

O >2 yards per hour

Even though I'm a **fish**, I **don't have scales.**
With my **dorsal fin,** I push myself **forward,**
and I **steer** with my **pectoral fins.**
I **don't have a tail fin.**

I swing **my tail** like
an **anchor** around a plant.
That way, I **don't drift away,**
and I stay calmly in my own
little area.

swims upright

I **can't swim fast,** but I **adapt my color**
to my surroundings. Nobody notices me
when I hang between the plants or the coral.
I **wait** until **something delicious swims past** and
suck it in with my snout lightning-fast.

People can catch me easily.
They're a **dangerous enemy.**
In Asia, they make **medicine**
out of seahorses. In other areas,
they use me in their artworks
or put me in an **aquarium**
because I look so special.

Best daddy
Just like with all seahorses,
daddy gets pregnant and
carries the fertilized eggs
of mommy.

Mommy and daddy are so in love! Daddy dances around mommy in the morning. They turn their tails around each other and start to hug. Sometimes, they change color and swim tail in tail over the bottom of the sea. Or they grab the same grass stem and sway together on the rhythm of the sea. Isn't that beautiful?

One day, mommy lets daddy know that she feels eggs in her belly. Snout against snout, they float upwards. Daddy sprays water out of his pouch to show that it's empty. Mommy pushes her ovipositor against his brood pouch and passes on hundreds of eggs like that. Her belly becomes thinner, and daddy's becomes bigger!

Afterwards, mommy swims away. The eggs continue tc grow in daddy's brood pouch. The pregnancy lasts approximately a month. Mommy comes to check on daddy every day to see how he's doing. The eggs in the pouch float in a liquid with food, adapted to their growth.

At full moon, daddy gives birth. That's a lot of work, because he pushes 100 to 200 seahorses out of his brood pouch! We're teeny-weeny (less than an inch long), but entirely full-grown. We swing our tails around each other and drift away in groups. We're free to start our own life!